THE SELF-TAUGHT CLARINET PLAYER

A GUIDE FOR MASTERING CLARINET TECHNIQUES

LOUISE LAWRENCE

Uptake publications

CONTENTS

A Wizwind inspiration

Uptake Publications

Taunton TA4 2AR

DEDICATION

Letters from the attic

Her appendix saved for me

Without her inspiration

Where would Wizwind be?

With grateful thanks to

the lady behind the mask.

INTRODUCTION

Why do I squeak? How can I make a better sound? Why do some notes sound weaker than others?

These frequently asked questions and many others are answered in *The Self-Taught Clarinet Player*, a useful little book to pop on your music stand and dip into when you pause for breath.

Embarking on any new instrument is an exciting adventure, but there are times when learning on your own can be a frustrating and lonely experience. Many adult learners have limited time to practise and are keen to get to the stage where they can just experience the joy of playing for pleasure. Rather than replicate the many tutor books already available, this guide highlights the most common technical issues you will encounter as a developing clarinettist and shows you how best to overcome them. Here you will learn how to make the most use of your practice time and get playing quickly. Hopefully, you will find this friendly little book interesting and fun.

Why the pictures? Because we all learn differently. An idea put one way can be baffling, put another can be obvious. I'm a visual learner. If an idea is given to me in picture form, I get it immediately and the message endures. Hopefully my quirky pictures will act as a trigger, reminding you of the points taught in the text.

This is the rough order of things:

Nuts and bolts of the clarinet itself: how best to set it up.

How to get the best sound: control of mouth, body and breath.

How to manage the instrument: control of hands, fingers and tongue.

Making best use of practice time: overcoming problems quickly.

Reading: becoming more fluent

Playing with others: understanding and mastering transposition and tuning.

Accessories: mouthpiece, reeds and maintenance.

Trouble-shooting: the type signalled by squeaks.

Oh yes, and ...

Back page - at the back of the book. You may want to read this page first.

Happy playing!

PRELIMINARY NOTE:

Throughout this book, left-handers: just reverse all the left and right directions.

1

INSTRUMENT PURCHASE
A BIT OF SAVVY AVOIDS DISAPPOINTMENT

Instrument Purchase – some thoughts:

It is really advisable to buy from a music shop specialising in woodwind instruments. Why? Because instruments usually come from the factory needing final preparations before re-sale – a job their specialist repairer will do. Your instrument will come with a warranty, and the shop's repairer will sort out technical issues. Non-specialist shops often send instruments away to get the job done – which means involving a third party and a frustrating wait for you.

There are plenty of sparkly new instruments available online, but best to be a bit savvy.

Some manufacturers cut corners in construction and/or use inferior quality materials – this will ultimately affect your progress. My instrument technician friends now refuse to work on cheap quality imports because they cannot be made to play well.

Second-hand instruments can be economic and successful if you can get your purchase to a teacher or repairer first.

Let them check it through for you before you commit to payment.

The best scenario is you could find a real gem; the worst is you could buy an instrument needing extensive overhaul or repair before it plays as it should. If you go the second-hand route, it's wisest and best to take advice.

2

REED SET UP AND ADJUSTMENT
THUMBNAIL

The way you set up your reed is vital: if the reed is not in the correct position it can affect the sound.

Select a reed and suck it three times, each time drawing it from the mouth slowly (like a lollipop stick).

Screw the mouthpiece onto the barrel - it's important to do this first because you can then attach the barrel to the rest of the clarinet without dislodging or damaging the reed.

With the mouthpiece hole facing, hold the barrel with your left hand.

Place the reed on the mouthpiece (shaped surface uppermost).

Hold the base of the reed with the left thumb.

With the right hand, adjust the reed so it is in line at the sides with just a thumbnail of black showing at the top. Never adjust the reed by pushing the tip.

Slide the ligature over the top of the mouthpiece, being careful not to catch the tip of the reed. Pull the ligature down, making sure you are not obscuring the curve of the shiny section of the reed, otherwise you will restrict is flexibility.

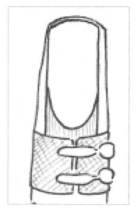

Thumbnail of black at the tip and curved base of the reed showing

You can now gently tighten the screws.

(Single screw ligatures just screw at the back on the right. Material ones often have holes in the fabric at the front - just be sure to get the holes absolutely central over the reed).

Screw securely, bottom screw, then top - but do not force.

TIP

If your reed is getting thin and worn out you can keep it going for a bit longer by putting it higher on the mouthpiece so that hardly any thumbnail of black is showing. It's a quick fix until you can pop a new one on.

For more information on reeds check **Chapter 24**.

3

PUTTING THE CLARINET TOGETHER
THE SAFE WAY

Think about this:

There are lots of keys on a clarinet. It's easy to bend them if you don't this properly.

Here's a simple way that avoids bending the keys. (NB - if you keep the corks greased then you should not have to force anything together).

Hold the lower joint with the left hand, gently clasping fingers over the two big metal cups at the bottom.

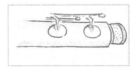

Two big metal cups

With your right hand, twist on the bell.

Transfer the lower joint to the right hand, gently clasping the fingers over those two big metal cups.

5

Cup the upper joint in the left hand, gently clasping fingers over the open holes and avoiding keys. The four tiny side keys on the upper joint should face you on top.

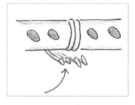

Four tiny keys

Twist the upper joint onto the lower joint, checking the connector key between upper joint and lower joint is in line.

Check that connector keys are in line

Now, with bell, lower joint and upper joint all connected together, cup the upper joint in the left hand as before (avoiding the keys), screw on the barrel. (NB - mouthpiece with reed should already be attached to the barrel, see **Chapter 2**). Twist the barrel around so that the reed is in line with the single finger hole and thumb rest at the back of the clarinet.

When you play, the reed will be on your bottom lip.

MOUTHPIECE POSITION - EMBOUCHURE

SKIN OF LIP

Skin of lip

Controlling the sound you make is hugely dependant on how much mouthpiece you use and where the reed sits on the lower lip (the embouchure).

Try this:

Place the index finger on your lower lip. Gently push all the fleshy red section of the lower lip over the lower teeth – *check on how this feels*.

NB - <u>this is too much bottom lip.</u>

Now place the index finger on the lower lip and repeat the exercise, but this time just pushing in *half* the fleshy red section of your lower lip – this feels like just the skin of the bottom lip – *check on how this feels*.

NB: <u>this is correct</u>

You have already set up the reed on the mouthpiece and it is connected to the barrel. So now, holding just the barrel (with mouthpiece attached) in your right hand, reed facing you, place the thumbnail of your left hand half way between the tip of the reed and the top of the ligature.

Place thumbnail half way between tip and ligature

With just the 'skin' of the lip over the teeth, slide the mouthpiece into your mouth until your thumb is against your chin.

Remove your thumb and place your teeth on the top of the mouthpiece. Relax your top lip - just let it drop down to close over the mouthpiece. Adjust and adapt the positioning slightly until it feels comfortable. The angle between the mouthpiece and the chin needs to be somewhere between 40 and 45 degrees.

· · ·

Draw your lips back as if you were tightening a washing line from either end.

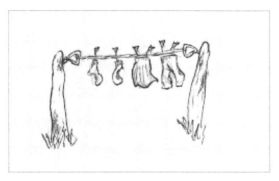

Draw lips back as if tightening a washing line from either end

Now, breathe heavily through the clarinet as if breathing steam on a window. This is the *correct breathing*.

Breathing is correct - *as if breathing steam on a window*

Blowing through the clarinet as if blowing out a candle results in puffed out cheeks. This is *incorrect* breathing.

Blowing is incorrect - as if blowing out candles

Check in a mirror that your cheeks are not puffed out. Done correctly, there should be slight dimples in your cheeks. Puffed out cheeks result in bunching of the bottom lip.

The bottom lip muscles control the flexibility of the reed, so it is important that they can work effectively. The shape of the cavity inside your mouth (which makes up your sounding box) will also be slightly altered, affecting the sound that you produce (see **Chapter 8**).

5

DIAPHRAGM BREATHING

ELEPHANTS AND BALLOONS

Make the most of your air. The diaphragm is like an elasticated rubber sheet resting between the rib cage and the stomach. Used well, you can take in more air and control how you let it out.

How does it feel?

Place your hand in front of your face.

Blow onto your palm and the air will feel cold. You are not using the diaphragm effectively. WRONG.

Breathe onto your palm and the air will feel warm. You are now using the diaphragm more effectively. RIGHT.

Now, place a hand on your stomach, just above your belly button and take in three short sniffs in close succession. You will feel your stomach puff up like a balloon.

Exercises to get started

Stand erect but relaxed with arms hanging by sides.

Imagine you are carrying a *heavy suitcase* in each hand - keep your back straight.

Weighty suitcase in each hand

Feel the weight on each shoulder - imagine an *elephant sitting on each shoulder*.

Elephant sitting on shoulders

Now, place your hand back on your stomach, remember as before - just above your belly button.

Make three short sniffs in close succession again - remember the feeling of the stomach puffing up like a balloon.

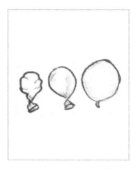

Stomach feels as if it is puffing up like a balloon

Relax, and let the air out. Repeat a few times.

Now try continuing the sniffs until your stomach feels fully stretched and full of air. Relax and let the air out. Repeat a few times.

Now open your mouth and LET the air into the stomach in one long swoop (stomach extends out).

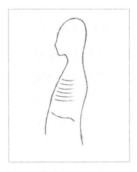

Stomach extends out as diaphragm muscle extends down sucking in air

LET the air out (stomach relaxes back).

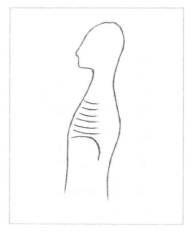

Stomach relaxes back as diaphragm pushes out air

Keep the elephants on your shoulders and repeat a few times.

(Just an aside here - the word 'let' is more useful than' breathe' in this exercise. The word 'breathe' usually triggers automatic reverting to default breathing habits. Interestingly, if you were to lie on the floor, you would find that your stomach extends outwards when you breathe in, and relaxes back as you breath out).

Now pick up the clarinet and take a long swoop of air into the diaphragm and breathe out through the clarinet on a bottom G.

Make sure that the elephants stay on your shoulders. *Check in the mirror. Your shoulders should not move.*

<u>Test it out</u>

Check how long your bottom G note lasts. You can do this breathing exercise (elephants and suitcases) anywhere and at any time. The more you exercise, the longer your bottom G will last and the more control you will have over your clarinet sound.

Caution:

If you feel light-headed, just take a break and come back to the exercise later.

6

POSTURE

TREE ROOTS AND PUPPETS

Breathing needs to be free and unrestricted. Fingers need to be loose and flexible. Aside from discomfort arising from repetitive strain, tension in neck, shoulders, upper-back and arms can inhibit breathing and swift movement of the fingers, so how you position your body in relation to the clarinet is important. Before working with the clarinet you need to be sure shoulders and arms are completely relaxed. Imagine you are a puppet. The strings holding up your arms have been cut so your arms hang loose by your sides. this concept will help you to avoid tension.

Keep your elbows slightly away from your sides.

The end of the clarinet should be held up slightly. An approximate 45 degree angle to the body will mean that you will have good flexibility in your arms and fingers, and optimise your control of the instrument. The sound will also project well.

Arms hang loose like a puppet with cut strings

Keep your legs comfortably straight and feet planted slightly apart. If you are securely attached to the floor, you will feel more in control of yourself and your instrument.

Flexible and grounded - like a rooted tree

Whatever situation you may be playing in, you will feel relaxed and flexible yet firm and grounded.

7

CONTROLLING THE TONE
TUBES OF SOUND

Everyone has their own clarinet sound – this is your clarinet voice. There are so many wonderful clarinet players out there - past and present, Klezmer, Jazz, Classical, Rock etc – all so different – personality comes into it a lot too. The more players you can listen to, the more ideas you will bring to your own playing. You will sub-consciously select the sound you want to make.

The **very best** way to improve your sound – long notes.

Choose a favourite low note. Take in air using diaphragm. Breathe through your clarinet to make a long steady note. Visualise this as a solid tube of sound.

A solid tube of sound

Keep it level - no wavering.

Choose a higher note and repeat.

Choose a lower note and repeat.

As you become a more adept Clarinettist, you can switch between higher and lower notes across the registers.

The more time you spend on long notes, the better your sound will be.

If you do this daily, you may think that your note tubes are getting more wavery, or that your sound is not improving. This is perfectly normal. Don't be disheartened. You are only becoming more aware and perceptive, which is the surest way to success.

You cannot help but improve by spending time on this activity.

8

OPEN NOTES

CHERRIES AND CATHEDRALS

Open notes

G, G sharp A and B flat are all called 'open notes' because many of the holes are uncovered. As you take your fingers off the holes, you are in effect making the instrument shorter and shorter. The sound can become thinner and less easy to control. These notes can sound weak in contrast to other notes and are more difficult to keep in tune.

Remedy:

Firstly, use a little more air. Now imagine a cathedral – large and spacious.

Resonating space - wide and spacious like a cathedral

Keep this visual image. You can make a bigger resonating space inside your mouth by opening out the throat slightly and lowering the back of the tongue – imagine placing a cherry on the back of your tongue whilst you play these open notes. (It should feel similar to stifling a yawn).

Cherry on back of tongue

Try playing notes in octaves, listening and adapting the air and tongue position to balance and match the sound. Remember to support well from the diaphragm:

Rich low 6-finger **G** - Yawning open **G**

Rich low 5-finger **A** - Yawning open **A**

Rich low 4-finger **B flat** - Yawning open **B flat**

NB

Playing can often sound 'lumpy', even if the fingers are fluent, simply because the sound isn't balanced across the registers.

9

POSITIONING THE FINGERS ON THE HOLES

FROG PADS AND HONEY POTS

The holes on the clarinet are large. It is important that they are covered completely so that no air escapes from the tone holes. Squeaking in the upper register is often caused by slight air leaks where one or more of the tone holes are not fully covered by the fingers. Keep the fingers floppy and relaxed –as if drumming the fingers on a table top.

Drumming fingers

Keep a curved hand position – imagine you are gently holding a ripe avocado in each hand.

Ripe avocado

Ensure the pads of the fingers are covering the holes. Visualise the finger pads of a frog.

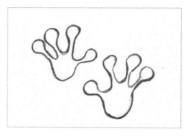

Frog's finger pads

You can test out whether your fingers are covering effectively in this way:

1. Gently but firmly cover the tone holes of the lower joint with the fingers of the right hand. Keep the left thumb on the thumb hole of the upper joint.

2. Gently plop the index finger of the left hand up and down. Listen very closely. You should hear a very satisfying 'plopping' sound.

3. Keep the index finger down. Now flop the second finger up and down....plop..plop..plop. Now the third finger...plop... plop...plop.

4. Now keep the upper joint holes covered with the thumb and fingers of the left hand. Plop the index finger of the right hand (there will be a slight key rattle with this one), plop the second finger, and then the third.

Pot of honey pouring out

Imagine you have poured a pot of honey down the clarinet. <u>Do not actually do this!</u> When you are covering the holes, imagine you are preventing honey from escaping from behind your fingers, but do not squeeze. Remember to keep that lovely firm, yet relaxed finger position.

10

FINGER STRETCHING
MOORHEN TOES

Notes can sound muffled or can squeak if the fingers do not fully cover the holes. Getting the fingers to move as you want means keeping control over them.

Try this for co-ordination:

First, hold up your left hand - palm facing away - as if saying 'Stop!'. Keep your fingers closed - now stretch your fingers open - then closed again.

Now try this:

1. Move just your little finger away from the other fingers and back.

2. Now, keeping little and ring fingers together, stretch them away from the other fingers, and back again.

Little finger and ring finger stretch

3. Now move little, ring and middle fingers out and back.

4. Now move just the thumb out and back.

Index finger and thumb stretch

Repeat the whole process with the right hand.

Now try the whole process with both hands at the same time – you'll find the co-ordination is easier.

Try this for greater stretch

Stretching fingers – visualise the stretched claws of a Moorhen and make your fingers do the same.

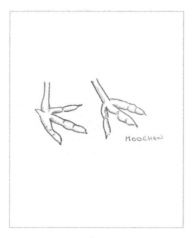

Moorhen toes

This exercise can be done under the dinner table when bored. Separate the little finger of of your left hand from the rest of the hand by stretching it across your knee. Continue the stretch - little and ring fingers together, middle and ring fingers together, repeating with your right hand.

11

TWISTING ON THE PIVOTAL NOTE

FIRE ENGINE

The position of the left index finger on the A key is really important. Get the movement to the A key right, and smooth movement from lower register to higher register notes (going across the break) will be *much, much* easier further down the line.

Try this:

Take the left hand off the clarinet and hold it out as if you were going to shake hands with a friend. Instead of shaking hands, imagine you are twisting a door knob.

Notice how the wrist and forearm move as one.

Place your left index finger on F$^{\#}$. Play the F$^{\#}$ and, in the same breath, using the 'door handle' twisting action, move the index finger off F$^{\#}$ and catch the A key with side of your index finger. Try and catch it just at the lower tip of the

Twist the door knob

key –the key is slanted down to make this easy. Twist back to the F# again.

Tip of the A key

Repeat this action over and over again in one breath – sounding like a fire-engine. Slur this exercise, do not tongue.

Fire engine

When this is easy move onto twisting to A from E, then D and lastly C.

Twisting to A

Check

Remember to make a long tube of sound whilst twisting. By doing this slurred, you can listen out for bumps or blips and work to get the finger work neat.

12

LEFT HAND THUMB POSITION
LEFT HAND WRIST TWIST

The left-hand thumb and the left-hand wrist work together:

Wrist:

Hold out your left-arm and re-run the door knob twisting action (**Chapter 11**).

Thumb:

The left-hand thumb position is important, not only to cover the tone hole at the back, but also for flexibility and seamless movement between the lower and the higher registers on the clarinet. Keep the thumb soft, floppy and relaxed - frog finger pads (**Chapter 9**) so the hole stays covered.

Check the angle between your thumb and the body of the clarinet. Ideally it should be at a 40 to 45 degree angle, like the angel of chin to mouthpiece and angle of clarinet to body.

When you do the testing exercise below, take this position as average and tweak slightly to get the optimum position for the length of your thumb.

Testing exercise:

Play a good rich sounding six finger bottom G – a long tube of sound, air supported from the diaphragm. Now move the little finger of the left hand slowly around a circuit of the left-hand little finger keys - G to E, G to F#, G to F. Keep going round and round.

Circular movement around the keys

Make sure you keep the wrist relaxed and loose, allowing the door knob twisting action to happen as you reach for the furthest keys. If your thumb is in the correct position, you should be able to move freely across all the notes without uncovering any of the tone holes. Once you can do this, try the same with the back register on – (the top notes are less forgiving): D to B, D to C#, D to C.

13

RIGHT-HAND THUMB
RIGHT HAND WRIST TWIST

As with the left-hand thumb and left wrist, the right-hand thumb and the right wrist work together:

Wrist:

Take the right hand off the clarinet and remind your self of the door knob twist action (**Chapter 11**), but this time working with the right hand and forearm. Now place your right-hand thumb under the clarinet thumb rest.

Thumb

The position of the right-hand thumb under the thumb rest is important. Too far forward and it will restrict the flexibility of movement of the right hand; too far back and it will feel insecure. Ideally it should be between the tip of the thumb and the thumb knuckle (where it bends).

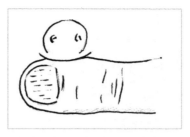

Thumb rest between knuckle and end of thumb

When you do the testing exercise below, take this as average and tweak slightly to get the optimum position for the length of your thumb.

Testing exercise:

Play that good rich sounding bottom G again – a lovely sonorous tube of sound. When happy, move the little finger of the right hand slowly around a circuit of the right-hand little finger keys G to E, G to F, G to G$^\#$, G to F$^\#$ - keep going round and round.

Circular movement round the keys

Make sure you keep the wrist relaxed and loose, allowing the door knob twisting action to happen as you reach for the furthest keys.

If your thumb is in the correct position, you should be able to move freely across all the notes without uncovering any of the tone holes.

Once you can do this, try the same with the back key on – (remember, the top notes are less forgiving): D to B, D to C, D to $D^{\#}$, D to $C^{\#}$.

14

THE REGISTER KEY

A MERE TWITCH

Following on from the correct left-thumb position (**Chapter 12**), the upper register notes can be reached by pressing just the very tip of the register key.

Tip of the register key

This is the tiniest, infinitesimal movement – little more than a controlled twitch. Watch your thumb do this and you will see how little the thumb needs to move before the key shifts to uncover the tone hole. The register key does not need to be pressed down fully to get the top notes. All you need to is create a tiny air leak on the clarinet and a top note will sound.

Try this:

Play your rich bottom G – six fingers floppy on the clarinet – *tube of sound*. Now just twitch the register key to get a top D and continue holding that top note.

Play a rich bottom A – five fingers floppy on the clarinet – *tube of sound*. Now just twitch the register key to get a top E and continue holding that top note.

Continue working on from B♭, C and any other note in the lower register that takes your fancy.

Tipping register key from low to high notes

NB

As you take more fingers off holes to create higher sounds you may have problems sustaining the notes. The next chapter will give you guidance on how to produce strong top notes.

15

STRONG AND SECURE TOP NOTES
ANCHOR - BE BRAVE

Anchoring the top notes

A strong, rich and secure sound in the lower register is an excellent anchor on which to build top notes. Moving on from the register twitching exercise in the previous chapter, you should find that top D, E and F are easy to hold, but if the notes break or squeak as you go higher, then check out the points below:

Increased air pressure:

Be brave and use plenty of air. Many people are scared of squeaking on the higher notes, and so they use less air. The reed needs to vibrate faster for the higher notes to sound. If you don't keep the pressure of air going through the clarinet, the reed will stop vibrating and there will be no sound.

Either that, or the reed will vibrate too slowly and you will just make a groaning sound.

Solution:

Visualise the solid tube of sound and use plenty of air support from the diaphragm - don't slacken off

Too much tension.

Sometimes the top notes won't sound at all. If you feel tense about playing higher, it is easy to start biting. This presses the reed against the tip of the mouthpiece and closes up the gap – the reed becomes constricted and the air can't get through to make it vibrate.

Solution:

Try putting a tiny bit more mouthpiece in your mouth, just to open things up. When you feel more secure, just keep the pressure of air up but ease the mouthpiece out again to a comfortable position that allows the top sounds to come through. You can make a rounder tone by imagining the cherry sitting on the back of your tongue (**Chapter 8**).

Not enough tension.

To keep the reed vibrating at a faster pitch, the bottom lip needs to be pulled taut.

Solution:

Imagine your lips as a washing line being pulled tauter at either end (**Chapter 4**). Keep the tube of sound solid, supporting from the diaphragm.

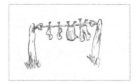

Washing line

The reed is too soft

The thinner the reed, the more flexible it is. This is not always a good thing. As you use more tension in the lower lip, a reed that is too thin will be pushed too close to the mouthpiece tip and restrict the air flow. Reeds also become thinner with age (acid in the saliva eats through the wood), so consider how long ago you changed your reed.

Acid can eat through the reed

Solution:

Put on a new reed. If you can't do this until later, then a good quick fix to keep you going in situ is to adjust the reed higher so that it is in line with the top of the mouthpiece with no 'thumb nail' of black showing. This really is just a short-term fix. If putting a new reed doesn't solve the problem, you may need to upgrade to a harder reed, (**Chapter 24**).

16

HANDS CLOSE

RELIEVING TENSION - DRUMMING

Watch any professional player and their fingers seem to hardly move. The more you move your fingers, the more likely they are to go down in the wrong place – not covering holes – catching other keys (squeak!) – and you will not be able to play quickly.

Try the finger plopping exercise (**Chapter 9**). Now start to squeeze all the fingers down on their holes. Then try moving the fingers of both hands up and down. They will feel sluggish and slow and you will feel tension in your forearms.

Now shake your left arm and then your right arm, and shake your left hand and then your right hand - roll your shoulders around. Drum the fingers of your left hand, then right hand on a table.

Drumming on a table requires relaxed fingers

Do the finger plopping exercise again (**Chapter 9**).

Try the fire-engine exercise (**Chapter 11**)

Try the left- hand little finger exercise (**Chapter 12**)

Try the right-hand little finger exercise (**Chapter 13**)

How close are your fingers?

17

TONGUING
OWL HOOTS

Tonguing is the technique of separating one note from the next with the tongue. Most beginners stop and start the note by blowing HOO HOO HOO, or opening and closing the throat, creating an OO OO OO sound.

Clarinet tonguing can be challenging for some more than others, depending on your tongue shape and the way that you pronounce words, but it is worth working on. A correct tonguing technique will produce a clear beginning to each note and allow you to play more quickly in the long-run.

Try this: (Whisper, no vocal chords):

OO OO OO (throat open and closes)

THOO THOO THOO (tongue flicks between teeth)

TOO TOO TOO (tip of tongue touches roof of mouth lightly)

DOO DOO DOO (area just behind the tip of the tongue touches roof of mouth with a slightly heavier action)

DOO DOO DOO, TOO TOO TOO or somewhere between the two will work for you.

Now try this:

Get a *solid tube of sound* going on a nice easy note. Now bring in the DOO/TOO action. The tongue acts like a tiny little hammer hitting the reed and separating the notes, chopping up that tube of sound into segments of tube – separate notes.

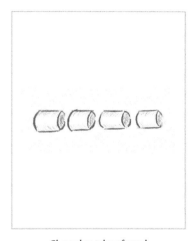

Chopped up tubes of sound

Every time the tongue hits the reed, it stops it vibrating. As long as you keep the tube of air going, the reed will vibrate again when the tongue moves away from the reed. The crucial thing is to keep that tube of air going as you tongue.

If this is all too tricky, try single notes - HOOD HOOD HOOD or HOOT HOOT HOOT. Next, move to continuous sounds -HOOD-HOOD-HOOD or HOOT-HOOT-HOOT.

Owl hoots

When you can do this, progress to DOODOODOO or TOOTOOTOO (NB - you are now starting the process with your tongue on the reed, so you will feel the pressure of air behind the tongue before the sound is emitted).

Once this starts to come, it's a question of listening and experimenting to get the clearest sound, minimising the sound that the tongue makes hitting the reed. You will end up with more of the note sound, and less tonguing sound - it will begin to sound more subtle and 'clean'. If you visualise the chopped up tube of sound, the gaps between the bits of sound are getting smaller.

18

SCALES

WHY BOTHER

Why play scales?

Because scales are the quickest way to learn all the most common finger moves we use in playing music.

Why don't people like playing them?

Because most people get frustrated.

They spend ages playing them over and over to get them right, and then when they come back to them later, they go wrong again.

Why does this happen?

Every time a scale goes wrong, your fingers are learning the wrong pattern.

If you play the scale over and over, getting it wrong, then you are training your fingers to play a wrong finger pattern – motor memory.

Playing a scale wrong is therefore actually worse than not playing a scale at all!

Why are wrong notes unsettling to hear?

Hearing a different sound to the one you are expecting can be an uncomfortable experience.

Solution

When learning a scale for the first time, play it so... so....slowly that you cannot possibly go wrong. It is best to read it from some kind of notation to start off with. Be sure to read the note and know what the fingering for that note is *before* your fingers move there. It is tempting to let the fingers take off and do their own thing.

If you do play a wrong note, correct it – go back to the beginning of the scale and play only as far as the offending note, but finishing on the corrected note this time. Stop. Play from the beginning again.

Do this three times and you will have re-trained your fingers so that they will get it right next time.

When you feel more secure with your scale, be content to play slowly and steadily. Imagine an elderly person plodding upstairs. You can upgrade to a more youthful jog when you are feeling even more confident.

Each stair the same space from the last

19

PRACTICE ROUTINE
WATCH TV

Little and often is best - you are likely to progress more quickly with just a few minutes each day rather than exhausting yourself with a three-hour session at the weekend.

Keep the clarinet accessible - invest in a clarinet stand and keep your instrument out on a stand rather than packed away in it's case. Playing a tricky bit of technique whilst the kettle's boiling, or a few scales while waiting for a phone call is a sure way to save time and move your playing on quickly.

Have a routine - playing long notes is the best way to start. Get control of the breathing and the embouchure. *Rich tubes of sound*. Next, scales and finger exercises - get control of the fingers. Then tricky sections of pieces (whilst the mind is still fresh). Lastly, whatever you fancy.

Vary the tasks - if you are bored with long notes, just do a couple and move onto something else. If you struggle with a scale or a tricky bit of music, don't keep going beyond the point of weariness or frustration - move on to playing something for fun.

Always try and bring in something utterly new – try new ways of doing things - new finger exercises and routines, new music.

Keep inspired and fresh - listen to other players and recordings and keep yourself open to new ideas.

Have specific targets to work towards – a 'performance' can be as understated as playing a tune to a friend. Aspirations to improve technique can be as humble as being able to play smoothly from one tricky note to another.

Take a break - if your concentration flags, take a break and do something entirely different. Watch tv, go for a walk, whatever, and amazingly enough, when you come back later you may well find the niggle you were struggling with has suddenly become easier.....your brain has been working on it whilst you were away from the clarinet altogether!

Take a break and watch TV

20

HOW TO PLAY TRICKY BITS

LOOKING AT THE WALL

Memorising is a valuable tool. By looking away from the music, you can really think about what your fingers are doing and train them quickly to do what you want.

Try this:

Circle the bit you can't play. If this is a whole line of notes, play slowly and work out which notes are the most difficult to move between. Narrow it down to the most challenging three notes, or maybe even just two. Play these notes very slowly from the music three times. Memorise these notes and play them again whilst looking at a blank wall.

Look at a blank wall

You have now trained your fingers to move with the correct finger pattern. Go back to looking at the music and add in *either* the previous note, *or* the note following, so you now you have four notes. Repeat the process with these four notes, playing from the page three times and then from memory three times. Continue the process, adding in notes one by one.

Messy blips - if you have tried this tactic but things still sound messy then try this:

Take each pair of notes in the phrase and listen carefully as you move between them. Check your fingers are moving together. If they move up or down at different times, then you will hear an extra note in between. Work out which finger is moving up or down <u>last</u>. Work slowly so to make that sluggish finger move up or down <u>first</u>. Now play the whole phrase and get a tad angry with the sluggish note. It will come out correctly because you are paying it extra attention and therefore anticipating it in advance.

Repeating wrong notes:

If you keep playing a wrong note in the same place, don't keep playing it wrong. You will be working the wrong fingering into your technique. Go slowly enough from the beginning of the phrase to get the offending note correct. Then repeat three times ending on the **correct** note. Remember – motor memory – training fingers to do what you want every time.

Keep a check on the state of your brain

This way of working is rewarding but very intense, so there will come a point when you'll feel tired and things start to fall apart. Maybe change onto a different type of practice now.

Play through something easy you enjoy, or walk away and do something entirely different. Your brain will still be mulling over the irksome problem. When you come back to it next time, you should find surprisingly that the awkward section is a lot easier.

21

READING MUSIC FLUENTLY
EYE HOPPING

If you listen to a young child learning to read, they hesitate between each word:

The.......cat.......sat.......on.......the.......mat

Big gaps

If you listen to an adult reading the same sentence, the words blend together:

Thecatsatonthemat

No gaps

Try reading the very first sentence on this page – the one in bold italics. Now read it again, but this time read it out loud. When you say the word 'listen', notice which word your eyes are focussed upon...probably on the word 'young' or 'child'. This is because we scan ahead with our eyes – and of course reading then becomes fluent. In the same way, *music* will sound more fluent if you can read ahead.

Eye hopping

<u>TIP</u>

Rather than resting your eyes on the longer notes when you play them, use the time to read ahead to the next note. You can use this strategy when you get to a rest, a breathing place and at the end of a line.

Consciously make yourself do this and eventually you will find yourself reading ahead on the shorter notes too. You'll continue to develop until you find yourself scanning ahead many notes at a time as you play.

22

TUNING
A TEAM GAME

Altering your pitch to play in tune with others is really important. However adept your playing, you won't gain popularity votes if you don't adapt your tuning to match your fellow players. Even when playing on your own, it is important to get used to playing at the correct pitch.

Tuning device

You can simply use a tuning fork, or you can download an App. You don't need anything complicated. There are plenty available at no cost. If you are going to invest in a metronome, then getting one with a tuner built in is even better.

Temperature

If the clarinet is warm, the pitch will be higher than if it is cold, so it is better to tune your instrument when it is warmed up. Rather than wait for this to happen gradually as you get playing, there is a quicker way:

Finger a bottom E so all the tone holes are covered. Breathe steadily through the instrument, air from the diaphragm. Push the air right through to the very end of the instrument whilst slackening off the embouchure so the reed does not vibrate and make a sound. This will produce a long huffing whisper down the instrument.

Tuning note

Now with the instrument warmed up, you can test your tuning note against your tuner. Tuning to a concert A is standard practice, so on Bb clarinet you would play an upper register B.

Tuning note B

Using this register for tuning will give you a more reliable guide than the B an octave lower because all the holes are covered, so it's less likely the pitch will waver with alterations in bottom lip pressure.

Length affects pitch – the tuning barrel

There are various ways you can alter the tuning, but first you need to check the barrel position on the upper joint. Play your tuning note B with the barrel pushed completely in. Now try pulling the barrel out so that there is a gap between the end of the barrel and the upper joint. There will be a small amount of the wood tenon showing.

A small amount of the wood tenon showing

Test your B again, and you will notice that the pitch is lower. The barrel section is designed to lengthen or shorten the clarinet and it's often referred to as the tuning barrel. By pulling out the barrel, you have effectively made the length of the clarinet longer so the air has to travel further. When testing your tuning, just pull the barrel out incrementally until the correct pitch is achieved. Always ensure the cork is well greased so you can adjust the barrel with ease.

Beware - no cork showing

If you pull out too far, you will be able to see the cork. This will make the clarinet play out of tune with itself. To hear this effect, try the following:

Push the barrel right in and play a bottom G, and then an open G.

Bottom G and open G

You should be able to match the tuning of the notes with slight adjustment of embouchure (see chapter 8 – Open Notes). Now pull the barrel out so you can see the cork. Try those two notes again and you will find that they are wildly out of tune and very difficult to match.

Confident and true

When you test for tuning, always use a good solid tube of sound. Project the air through in a steady stream, with breath level and sustained by the diaphragm. Your tuning note needs to be played confidently. Playing tentatively can raise the pitch, and over blowing can lower the pitch. You should not have to tighten or slacken the embouchure to match up, just a default position sufficient to play an easy relaxed note is fine.

Maintaining pitch while playing

Your instrument is now correctly pitched, but as you get more proficient you'll notice some notes need tweaking to keep them in tune in relation to the rest of the instrument. Get in the habit of listening to your tuning during practice sessions, and when playing with others. This is easiest to check when you come to any long notes within a phrase. Tighten the embouchure (tennis net taut), and you will raise the pitch, relax the embouchure (tennis net slack) and the pitch will drop. Players often refer to this as 'lipping up' or 'lipping down'.

Anticipating pitch

When you are just starting out, adjusting the position of the barrel and keeping good control of air and embouchure will stand you in good stead. With experience you will start to automatically match your embouchure to an internalised sense of pitch. This is a very necessary skill that will develop naturally over time if you just listen and stay aware.

Hearing notes in your head before you play them brings about instinctive and involuntary subtle changes to the mouth cavity – changes that are needed to create the pitch you are aiming for. You can test this out by singing a low note and then a high note in your head and noticing how this feels. You may want to revisit Chapters 7 and 8 and remind yourself of the cherry and the cathedral.

Tongue position

I know that by varying the position of the back of my tongue, I can maintain a round sound and adjust my pitch. This feels like a slow motion 'yaaa' type movement when opening out, and relaxing the 'yaaa' when adjusting back. This is particularly noticeable when playing with others because in an ensemble situation the pitch is never static, so it's a question of staying aware, listening and adapting all the time to blend in. While players agree that keeping the throat open and relaxed is important, most say adjustments within the mouth have become so innate and automatic over time that they are unaware of the tongue position while playing. Some texts talk about 'flattening the back of the tongue' to help general sound production, particularly when playing at the outer ranges of the instrument. This is where the concepts of cherry and cathedral should help. It would be interesting to study MRI scans to gain some insight on the subject. Just getting into the habit of listening to your tone and tuning every time you play will develop your aural awareness. This will guide any subtle adjustments you'll need to make to tune in to others.

· · ·

Quick check list overview:

- Check barrel position
- Maintain air pressure
- Lip tension – be aware and adapt as needed
- Jaw tension – be aware and adapt as needed
- Pitching - adjusting the back of the tongue if needed

All instruments have their idiosyncrasies too, so knowing your instrument and which notes have a tendency to play slightly sharp or flat is part of the whole tuning experience.

Barrel length – wood and plastic clarinets:

A wooden clarinet will take longer to bring up to pitch than a plastic instrument because the material is more dense. If you purchase a wooden clarinet, it is likely to come with a standard length barrel (65 or 66 millimetres) and a shorter barrel. The short barrel is particularly useful if you are playing with an ensemble and struggling to get up to pitch at the outset. You can start on the short barrel and switch to the longer barrel as the clarinet warms.

23

TRANSPOSITION

THE CLARINET IS A TRANSPOSING INSTRUMENT

There are various members of the clarinet family, but for the purposes of this chapter we'll consider the Bb clarinet because this is the instrument most commonly played.

The Bb clarinet is a transposing instrument. What does this mean?

Imagine there are four musicians in a room playing the following instruments:

Keyboard, violin, flute, and Bb clarinet

Everyone reads the note C

Everyone reads the note C

The note you'll hear on keyboard, violin and flute is C.

The note you'll hear on clarinet will be Bb, one note lower (a tone, to be precise). The clarinet therefore needs to play a D (one note higher) to pitch a C, (referred to as 'concert pitch'), along with everyone else. This is why the clarinet is referred to as the Bb clarinet.

This means that Bb clarinets cannot play from the same music and sound the same as keyboard, violin, flute or any other non-transposing instrument, they will sound a note lower. The clarinet needs to play everything up one note (one tone) to sound the same. When non-transposing instruments play in the key of C major, the clarinet has to play in the key of D major. The key signature of the clarinet music needs to be adapted.

If you purchase music with a keyboard accompaniment, the clarinet part will be transposed for you.

See some examples below:

Examples of keys transposed from keyboard to clarinet

NB – these are only some of the key signatures, and any accidentals will need adapting. The remit of this book is to cover technique rather than theory, but here's a nifty trick that simplifies the key signature alteration process that you need. Take a look at the line below. Flats are cumulative to the left, and sharps cumulative to the right. Therefore if the piano is in G major (one sharp), you move along two to the right where there are now three sharps, so the clarinet will be in the key of A.

If you check this against the examples given, you can see that it works.

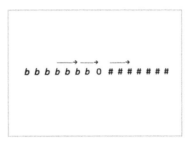

Flats cumulative to the left, and sharps to the right. Hop along two to the right to find the key signature for the clarinet

Clarinets in other keys

As mentioned before, there are various members of the clarinet family, but it is worth noting that whichever clarinet you play, the fingering will always correspond to the same written note. Whether you are playing Eb, C, A, Alto, Bass or Contrabass clarinet, if you see the note C in the lower register (the chalumeau register), it will be fingered with the three fingers and thumb of the left hand. This is just to simplify things, otherwise clarinettists would have the overwhelming task of having to change fingering patterns whenever they switched between the variously pitched instruments!

Ultimately, as a clarinettist, learning to transpose at sight is an invaluable skill because you'll have the independence to play with whoever, whenever.

24

MOUTHPIECE, LIGATURE AND REED
KEEP IT SIMPLE

Mouthpiece

You may have a top-of-the-range-clarinet, but it will be difficult to make a good sound if you have an inferior mouthpiece. By contrast you can have just a basic student clarinet and make a good sound if you have a good mouthpiece.

There are many mouthpieces on the market to choose from with different characteristics, but it is best to keep simple at the outset.

A *Yamaha 4C* is an excellent inexpensive starter mouthpiece. You can always upgrade when you have gained enough technical control to really notice the difference in tone, as well as the listening experience to know what sound you want to create.

Ligature

A standard metal ligature with screws at the front is fine – but beware, some cheap quality ones can keep sliding off the mouthpiece, dislodging the reed. Be sure your ligature will hold in place as you tighten the screws. The fabric or leather type with the screws at the back is slightly easier to set up.

There are many ligatures on the market, and some clarinettists believe the type of ligature you choose can make a significant difference to the sound you make. It is an individual thing and, as with the mouthpiece, it's best to keep your choices simple and functional until your playing has progressed further.

Reed

The lip muscles will be weaker and under-developed when you start playing the clarinet, so you need a reed which is thin and will vibrate easily with little resistance.

Reeds come in different thicknesses, the lower the number, the thinner the reed. There are many brands on the market and costs vary, but a poor quality reed will never give you a good sound.

Rico reeds (orange box) work well for beginners. Strength **1.5** is a good starting place. As you venture into the upper register and your lip muscles firm up you can progress up to a **2** strength.

Royal reeds (blue box) are slightly more expensive, but better quality.

Once you have gained control of the upper register, keep assessing the sound you make. If you wish, you can then experiment with a harder reed, but take your time. It does not necessarily follow that the more experienced the player, the harder the reed. There are many professionals who find they can get the flexibility, resonance and roundness of tone they need on a softer reed.

Comfort and physicality play a part too. As with ligature and mouthpiece, reed choice is very much a personal preference. These are all aspects to consider further down the line as you tweak your 'unique clarinet voice'.

25

ACCESSORIES
BE PRUDENT

Think about this:

As with any new hobby, there are so many products out there to tempt you. Best not indulge until you have been playing a while and know what you will really need. However, generally speaking, it's better to spend rather more for a good quality product to ensure it will do the job properly.

Useful accessories that really make a difference:

Clarinet cleaner/swab: – essential for cleaning – get a good quality absorbent one – not the felt variety.

Mouthpiece steriliser: – prevents germs collecting in the mouthpiece.

Cork grease: – essential for keeping joints lubricated so they don't stick.

Bore oil: – **Only** if you have a wooden Clarinet – prevents wood drying out and splitting.

Mouthpiece patch: – rubber pad that sticks to the mouthpiece – eases vibration on teeth and makes playing more comfortable – the thicker variety is best.

Thumb rest cushion: – slides onto the metal thumb rest at the back of the clarinet and saves you from suffering a sore thumb – the soft rubber type is more effective than the hard.

Clarinet sling: – takes the strain off the right hand – less weight on the thumb – eases repetitive strain. Most types hook into the hole on the metal thumb rest. If there is no hole on your thumb rest, make sure the sling you buy comes with a slotted leather strip so that it will still attach.

Clarinet stand: – keep the clarinet on a stand and you'll pick it up and play more regularly – there is a collapsible design that stores in the bell.

Music stand: – better than straining neck to read at an angle – it will improve your playing position. The collapsible type is great for getting out and playing with others.

26

CLEANING AND MAINTENANCE

CIGARETTE PAPERS - HOW TO KEEP YOUR CLARINET HEALTHY

Cleaning your clarinet:

Use a good quality clarinet swab – avoid the cheap felt strip variety – it won't absorb moisture. Take the clarinet apart, pull the swab through each section including the mouthpiece, and dry off the reed.

Cleaning the mouthpiece:

Fill a sink with **cold** water (hot water will discolour the mouthpiece), and a tiny drop of washing-up liquid. Hold by the cork (do not immerse the cork), and gently clean with a soft toothbrush. Rinse with cold water and dry. Spray the mouthpiece with mouthpiece steriliser after.

Stiff joints:

Keep the corks lubricated and it will be easier to put your clarinet together. If the corks get dry, then the keys can bend with forcing. Just dab some grease on the cork and work it in with your finger. Be careful to wash your hands afterwards so the cork grease doesn't collect in the tone holes when you play.

Sticky pads:

Cigarette papers (used because they are absorbent but non abrasive). Place one sheet between the pad and the hole it covers. Press down gently on the metal cup holding the pad whilst drawing the cigarette paper out. This cleans the sticky residue off the pad.

Bubbling sounds:

Look for a hole that is wet. Open the key to uncover the hole. Whilst the hole is uncovered, blow a fast jet of air between the open hole and the body of the clarinet to get rid of the excess moisture. Place a sheet of cigarette paper between the pad and the hole it covers. Very gently, press down on the metal key. Open the key and move to a fresh, dry section of paper and press down again. Keep repeating until the paper has absorbed all the water and comes out dry.

Bore Oil: – (wooden clarinets only).

Use very sparingly. Put a few drops on your clarinet swab every three or four months and just continue to clean with the swab as usual. The oil works into the wood and helps to prevent the wood drying out and splitting.

Tip:

Avoid eating and drinking before playing to avoid sticky pads.

27

SQUEAKS

A SUBSTANTIAL LIST!

With experience you get to recognise the different kind of squeaks

Squeak!

Reed broken - never adjust the reed by pushing the tip/beware of catching it on clothing.

Reed worn out – if you've had it on for more than two weeks try changing it (**Chapter 15**).

Reed too soft – if you've been playing on the same strength reed for a while, you may need to upgrade to a higher strength, ie: thicker reed (**Chapter 24**).

Reed too dry – take it off and give it a suck.

Reed in wrong position – check it is in line and that there is a finger nail of black at the top (**Chapter 2**).

Reed warped – check the tip. If it's wrinkled, take it off and give it a suck, then place it on a clean, flat surface - shaped surface uppermost. Press the sloped area down with your thumb fairly firmly, and draw the reed back slowly from under your finger, (you may need to do this a few times). This will iron out any warping.

Mouth in wrong position – check skin of lip (**Chapter 4**).

Cheeks puffing – check in mirror – steamy window breath, not candle blowing, washing line tension (**Chapter 4**).

Too much mouthpiece – edge the mouthpiece out a bit (**Chapters 2 and 15**).

Fingers not covering holes – check finger plopping action and remember to keep fingers relaxed. Check fingers are stretching enough – moorhen toes (**Chapters 9 and 10**).

Fingers catching keys –check left and/or right index fingers are not catching the clarinet side keys.

Check curved hand position – avocado shape (**Chapter 9**).

Finger tension – relax – put the clarinet down and shake your hands, roll your shoulders around and shake your arms. Drumming fingers (**Chapter 16**).

Fault on the instrument – do a vacuum test. Check the upper joint. Holding only the upper joint with your right-hand, place your left-hand fingers on the holes and your thumb on the back hole so that all the holes are covered. Now place the end of the clarinet joint on the ball of the right-hand so that the tube is sealed and suck hard on the remaining open end of the joint. A vacuum should build up. Pull the right-hand away and you should hear a satisfying popping sound.

Check lower joint in the same way – holding just the lower joint with your left-hand, place your right-hand fingers on the holes and depress the low E key with your right-hand little finger. Now place the end of the clarinet joint on the ball of your left -hand and repeat the 'suck and pull' action listening for the popping sound.

If popping sounds don't happen, one or more of the pads may not be covering the holes. Check out with a repairer.

28

BACK PAGE

READING FROM THE END BACKWARDS

It is an odd fact that mistakes often happen at towards the end of a piece of music. Here are some possible reasons why.

Typical practice habit

Most people start at the beginning (an obvious place to start). They go wrong, start again, go wrong, start again, etc, etc, etc.

The end of the piece rarely gets played

The beginning gets played many times, but the end of the piece rarely gets reached - so that section doesn't get played very often - it's not very familiar.

Concentration diminishes

Most people are more alert at the beginning of a task. We take for granted the simultaneous skill of reading music with the coordination involved in playing an instrument. This requires a huge amount of concentration.

Anxiety increases

As you venture into uncharted territory, the likelihood of going wrong is greater.

Solution:

Start practice session with the end of the piece.

THE END

ABOUT THE AUTHOR

Louise graduated from the London College of Music with ALCM and LLCM and, after a further teaching qualification took the post of Woodwind teacher for North Devon LEA. Since her subsequent post as clarinet and saxophone tutor for Blundell's School, Louise's ongoing freelance work in Somerset has involved teaching people of all ages and performing with a variety of Classical, Jazz and Klezmer ensembles.

Her music projects have been many and varied. They include co-founding the *High Park Community Music School* which enables any child to play music; forming the adult band *Hoot* which moves adults towards improvisation; and collaborating on *The Mosaic of Art and Vision* workshops designed to teach children how to create art inspired by music.

Since gaining a B.Sc (Hons) in Psychology, Louise has been developing *Wizwind*, an innovative teaching method that fast-tracks music learning for people who struggle to read music, and liberates people who struggle to play without music.

During the lockdown of 2019, fellow players trekked to the remote farm in Somerset, where Louise lives, to rehearse in a large barn, warmed by a fire pit and overlooking fields of bemused cattle. Playing music with others during such a challenging time seemed such a joyous privilege. The Self-Taught Clarinet Player (the first in the Self-Taught series) was inspired by a realisation there could be many people embarking on learning the clarinet online, and that some insights from a friendly clarinettist might encourage and spur on the lonely blower.

Other *Wizwind* publications can be found on Louise's website:

www.wizwind.co.uk

Milton Keynes UK
Ingram Content Group UK Ltd.
UKHW020638151123
432615UK00018B/793